Edited by John N. Critchley
Designed by Ann M. Pianta
Printed in Singapore
through Palace Press
San Francisco, California
ISBN 0-930527-18-6

Published by Foremost Books
A division of Embassy Imprint, Inc.
Old Saybrook, Connecticut 06475 U.S.A.
1-800-999-1075

Overleaf: Everglades at Dawn

FLORIDA'S
Gulf Coast

Photographed by Clyde H. Smith

Published by Foremost Books
A division of Embassy Imprint, Inc.

Recollections of the Sunshine State

There was a time for me, as a youngster back in the 1930's and 1940's, that going to Florida was a grand adventure filled with many new discoveries! Our country was coming out of the depths of the Great Depression and jobs were scarce. My father's position as a fire watcher for the forest service in New England was suspended in the winter months when the threat of fire diminished. In those days, having a "job," no matter what, meant survival as well as self-esteem. There was no welfare system that suited my family's situation, and like many others of the time we scratched for a living wherever we could find it.

Florida, with its enticing warm climate and plentiful job opportunities beckoned. So, with the climax of each autumn season in New England, the stage was set for our annual migration south. We crammed all of our worldly goods into the rumble seat of our model "A" Ford. Stuff was even lashed in crates on the running boards and a big box projected from the rear spare tire. Somewhere within the massive pile there was even a niche for our part-collie family dog, "Glory." As I was traveling the highways and byways to bring you these photographs, I realized that many of my most cherished memories as a young boy are those of my winter trips to Florida's Gulf Coast..

Our route followed the only major highway of the time – the eastern seaboard's U.S. Route 1 – which was still a dirt road in many places. It twisted and turned through every obstruction and major metropolis along the way. There were many railroad crossings – a big thrill for me to see giant steam engines straining by with pullman cars or counting miles of box cars while waiting for the caboose. Not so much fun for my dad, however, who was anxious to get up to cruisin' speed – which was all of 30 mph! The entire journey under the best of conditions took up to ten days, longer if there were storms, mud slides, or washouts.

Nearing the Florida State Line was always a time of exciting expectations – our wistful dreams of sunshine, sandy beaches, and orange juice must be just around the corner. But it was not juice that greeted us at the border. Instead we came upon a clutter of roadside stands selling gingerbread and buttermilk! I haven't the foggiest notion why this stuff was so popular, but I remember it was always a big treat for my father. Not me!

At last, away to the sandy beaches, right? Well not quite. Remember that the Interstate Highway system had not yet been invented, and was in fact decades away from development. U. S. Route 1 dropped due south toward Jacksonville. But we were pioneers off to parts unknown and the Gulf Coast. The long diagonal route here was a seemingly interminable dusty lane through stringy pine barrens and palmetto scrub. We trundled along through this inhospitable land for miles on end, sometimes without seeing another soul. There always seemed to be brush fires burning along the roadway. Wild creatures seeking safe refuge from the burning brush were often driven to the highway. Chugging along in our model "A" between herds of deer, wild pigs, alligators, snakes and lizards was quite an experience. Once when we slowed for a gang of baby pigs, our dog Glory bolted in hot pursuit. The little guys scurried into a palmetto thicket and suddenly mama pig came charging out in search of the tormentor! She was a formidable razorback hog with bristling hair and yellow fangs. Glory made a flying leap into the rumble seat and away we went to safety. That really made an impression on me, and on the dog, too, I'm sure.

On another occasion my mother tells me the story of cruising down the highway when, without warning, the rear wheel of our car came loose and went rolling by the car. Not just the tire, but the entire wheel. My parents shifted to balance the vehicle as it kept going on three wheels, and watched in disbelief as the wheel bounded across a field and crashed into someone's shack. The surprised occupants ejected from the building as if shot out of a cannon, and the wheel came to a spinning stop on their kitchen floor.

We lived in many different places each winter. One especially memorable time was a winter we lived in Sarasota. My route to and from school passed by the winter quarters of the Ringling Brothers Circus. Known as the "Greatest Show on Earth," the circus had a magnetic attraction and I stopped by after school at every opportunity. I made friends with some of the performers who were often practicing acrobatic tricks or trapeze acts. There was a tight rope for beginners – about one foot off the ground – and I was allowed to try my skill at walking it while a pretty young circus girl held my hand! My greatest joy was riding the back of an elephant while it pulled long poles used to erect the big top. A crew of men practiced for raising the tent and driving stakes. "My" elephant was part of the crew and trudged along doing the heavy work with its trunk. Can you imagine letting a young boy ride a working elephant today? It really was a simpler time.

I took my very first airplane flight over the Gulf Coast of Florida in 1935. The aircraft was a tri-motored Ford and I was about five years old. My mother recalls that every passenger was charged by weight. One penny per pound for a half hour of flying time. I was kind of skinny so my ticket cost all of 44¢.

Flying is still one of the best ways to see Florida, but I doubt there's any place where they charge by the pound anymore. While doing photography for this book along Florida's Gulf Coast, I spent a lot of time in the air re-acquainting myself with old familiar places. Sure, things have changed a lot. But in spite of the development that we associate with progress, there is still a lot of wild and remote land out there. If you don't believe it, take a little flight toward some of the interior or the offshore mangrove islands. There are still many adventures and new discoveries waiting for you in the Sunshine State.

Clyde H. Smith

Overleaf: Tampa at night

Overleaf: Sanibel Island

Bambusa Oldhami

12

Flamingo

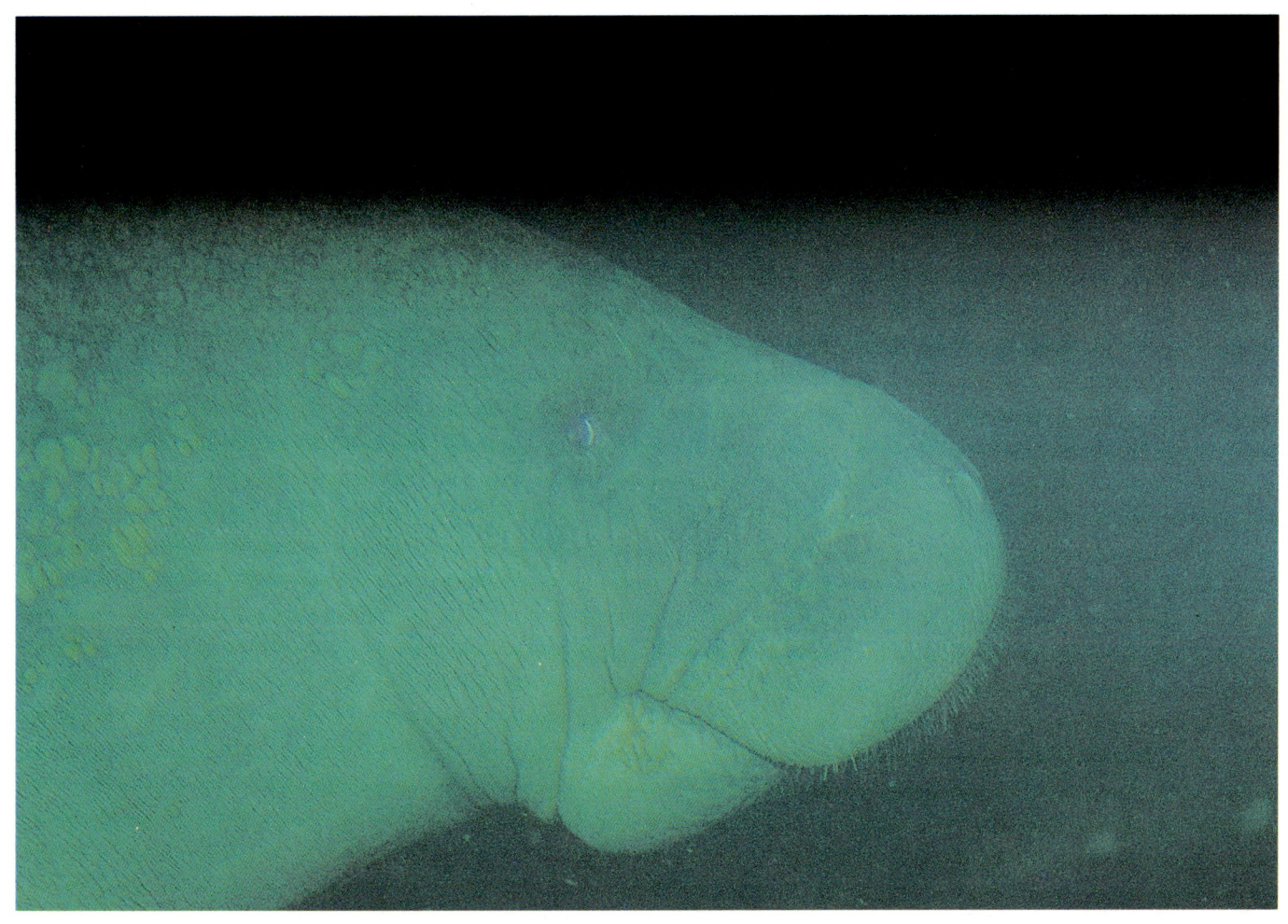

Great White Heron Wildlife Refuge
Manatee

Anhinga

Laughing Gulls

Sea Grapes

Seashells at Captiva

Overleaf: Don Caesar Resort

Morning Stroll   Perdido Beach

Man- of- War

Beach Art

Waiting for the "Green Flash"

Fort Pickens State Park

Gulf Islands National Park

Gulf Islands National Park

Overleaf: Sand Key Lighthouse

Tuna Tower

Panama City

Intracoastal Waterway at Pensacola

Schooner at Key West

Pensacola Lighthouse

Approaching Charlotte Harbor

Big Lagoon

Apalachicola

Overleaf: Sarasota at night

Van Weyzal Performing Arts Hall

Tallulah and friend

Bok Tower Gardens   Base of Bok Tower

Sarasota

Sarasota

State Capitol - Old and New

Old State House Cupola

Overleaf: Dawn at Big Lagoon
State Park

St. Petersburg

Sunrise

Business

Pleasure

Sponge Boutique

Shops at Key West

Sponge Divers at Tarpon Springs   Tarpon Springs Tribute

Overleaf: Sandhill Cranes
    at Myakka River State Park

Sunrise near Pensacola

Egret

Great Blue Heron   Apalachicola River dividing Time Zones

Rainbow

Hawk

J.N. "Ding" Darling National Wildlife Refuge
Sanibel Island

Anhinga

Overleaf: National Audubon Society Wildlife Refuge
at Corkscrew Swamp

Blazing Sunset

Alligator

Ichetucknee Springs State Park

Manatee Springs State Park

Fishing Laws

Law-Abiding Heron

Corkscrew Swamp Sanctuary

Myakka River State Park inhabitant

Overleaf: Seven Mile Bridge

Eden Gardens State Park

Orchids at Selby Gardens

Kumquat

Visit from "Alfie," a Great Blue Heron
Holmes Beach

Ca' d' Zan - The Ringling Home
Sarasota

Courtyard - Ringling Museum of Art

Overleaf: Myakka River State Park

Sugarcane in Blossom

Sugarcane Harvest

St. Agatha's Episcopal Church
DeFuniak Springs

Old Barn near Fort White

Caloosahatchee River Canal
LaBelle

Cruising the Waterway

Orange Grove

Orange Grove Etiquette

Overleaf: University of Tampa

99

University of Tampa

Big Cypress Swamp
Seminole State Park

Pensacola Naval Air Station

National Museum of Naval Aviation
Pensacola

Gulls at Sunset

Portable Radar - Key West

Clearwater

Gulf of Mexico   *Overleaf*: Outer Islands at Mouth of Tampa Bay

Brown Pelicans

Flamingo Marina
Everglades National Park

Starfish

Marooned Dingy - Gulf Islands

Snowy Egret

Morning Beachcombers

Last Cast

Boca Grande

Overleaf: Florida Intracoastal Canal
near Lake Okeechobee

Marco Island

Causeway to St. George Island

Sailor's Delight

10,000 Islands

Route 292 - Perdido Key
Intracoastal Waterway Bridge

Great Blue Heron

White Pelicans - Bradley Key
Everglades National Park